DEATHS THAT TRAVEL WITH THE WEATHER

DEATHS THAT TRAVEL

WITH THE WEATHER

LOUIE SKIPPER

ORCHISES WASHINGTON 1992

Library of Congress Cataloging in Publication Data
Skipper, Louie, 1950-
  Deaths that Travel with the Weather / Louie Skipper.
    p. cm.
    ISBN 0-914061-29-1 : $25.00 -- ISBN 0-914061-24-0 (pbk) : $10.00
  I. Title.
PS3569.K54D4   1992
811'.54--dc20   91-26642
                                                        CIP

ACKNOWLEDGEMENTS
Portions of this work have previously appeared in the following publications: *Barataria Review, The Black Warrior Review, The Kenyon Review, The New Virqinia Review, Poetry Miscellany, Quarterly West,* and *The Reaper.* Sections of the poem also appeared in *Alabama Poets* and in a chapbook, *Small Song of the New Moon.* Grateful acknowledgement is made to the Alabama State Council on the Arts, Vermont College, and the Bread Loaf Writers' Conference. I especially thank Ed Haworth-Hoeppner, the late Everette Maddox, Larry Moffi, Dennis Sampson, James Seay, the Rt. Rev. Furman C. Stough, and Leslie Ullman for their friendship and encouragement.

Published by Orchises Press
P. O. Box 20602
Alexandria
Virginia
22320-1602

G 6 E 4 C 2 A

for Stephanie

and Stephen

I perish by this people which I made.
— MORTE D'ARTHUR

Deaths that Travel with the Weather

Do not confuse the chronology of the life
with the chronology of the art:
                                even in death

    there is vanity. When I was five
    I watched as they wheeled off

    the old man who lived
                      next door

    on Edgewood Drive, Grandaddy John,

    dead for days before they found him,
    his legs straight out,
                face black from lack of breath.

          Winter nights
he creaked through my house, staggering
from the crypt that had closed behind him.

    I heard him climbing from underground
    to shudder with the heat out the furnace floor grate,
    smelling like the shine on a pair of shoes,

the color of my mother's blackest dress.
                                          Or he held out
    in the gleam of the tense piano,

when he wasn't drawn by the light of the freezer door,
mastered by his own death,

                alive in anything
that squared to the humped, long shape of his plot.

            Out of the tomb he took to,
        he rose from his encumbrances

    toward wherever in the house he could find me alone.
    Yet no motion the old man made

    could return me to his house again.
    All the lives I still lived put him off
                                        and he ranted
that no place was set for him at the dining room table
and no one called his name aloud or thought to ask how he was.

    The last night I caught him,

            his disposition reduced
    to putting our dog up to a howl,
                                he roared away.

    I went on my own after him,
                            muttering words

    I learned would drive him off. He lay down with me

and the longer dead at night beside the still waters
but I found no comfort in that shadow

    and feared no evil like Grandaddy John
    watching me burn like hellfire into the visible.

    It was my grandmother
                    I heard from the living room
    playing *Leaning on the Everlasting Arms*
    that last time I saw him large in darkness

        when he took to the skies,
    proud of me.

    Liking the love I have only for myself,
    I have to confess

    I learned from him how prayers
            are ways of begging
    for revenge.

Looking for him so long ago in the sky
I began to see why it matters how the story begins,

    always with our helplessness singling us out
    on our own

    away from the love of God
    that is really just the passage of time
            darkened by death
taking us farther than we want to go.

Now I understand the sparrow,

how it tried to take the pane

between the hospital waiting room and the rest of the sky,
the sparrow that struck the glass

then fell back,
stunned.

I understand why
for a time it held to a nearby limb:

All you
who must be patient,

parted from those you love
by the good health that takes you to your feet,

consider
in random spaces

between your life
and the balance you wait for each doctor to bring,

the sparrow,
his odds against mistaking
for something solid
the sense of freedom that comes
from flight.

IN 1962
>   when stories of the world were told
>   of a little girl murdered in our town,

>   of the lumberjack down the street
>   beating his wife, or of the teenager next door

> sent away to bear her secret child,
>   I heard how Jake Buchanan,

> a man too big for words,
>   fumbled over the telephone

>   through promises
>   he hoped would win his wife again.

>   And I had it explained,
>   how, his temper lost, point-blank,

> he shot himself between the eyes while she listened on the line.
>   When a grave was dug in late winter rain

> they crowded Jake and Sable
>   a final time under opened black umbrellas.

> A preacher struggled for us all beside the grave of Jake's making,
>   and the ladies paid their last respects
>   in prayers Jake refused to hear

>   as his widow, no longer married for awhile,
>   fell into a car and drove away.

>   Now and again over twenty-seven years
>   I catch myself beside Jake's claim.

I would like to tell him the earth is too full
        of those who once called me home.

        I heard for myself
how doctors strongarmed Jake

                then left his wife
        holding his hand and watching while he died.

No matter what events were found out
and staggered in

        off the street
from Selma, Cuba, and Berlin,
                        Russian missiles pointed at our house,
or freedom riders singing their way through black-belt towns
        with Alabama names,

Cornelia would ask, and Quilla answer
to any right or wrong,

                        dressed in Sunday clothes
with hats as big as platters.

                Mornings began with questions
and reports on Cluster's younger husband, Otho,
        who came home late again from playing the blues.

Then, in the end, they were face up,
side to side

across a hundred yards:
the rough husband who kept his vows

                    and told his wife
where she could go then how to stay away
    in silence

deeper than the two old ladies keep near his side.
At night they would give the news

                    between their plots
in the half-life of a cricket

                rejoicing in the tension
the air takes on a little before it rains,
    the tension in my hands they once took into their own.

There is an absolute over all I see.
Above their lengths figure crosses,

                        the dates they kept,
what little truth watches me here,

                        the stories they told
of a wife extending her will too far
    while God revealed what anger was,

of a girl next door who fell into temptation,
    was shamed, and moved away.

                Were they so wrong
to confuse sin with the lives that suffered before them?

                                                We

reach out as our lives stand alone under watchful eyes.
    Some will always say

they find they are naked there
under the tree of knowledge.

                         And I know that Quilla
would point out

                how even the black branches of the forbidden tree
strain
    like the hand of God turned away,

putting behind Him
once and for all

                the paradise of His first rejection,
although I still wonder over sin,

                         the perfect marriage
to yearn with the dead for whatever the stars will throw away.
    No matter how we reason

the truth is we do not last.
I remember wondering what was the point

                                 the girl next door
in high heels had to make.

I remember wondering what was the point to the blues.

And what comes to mind
is a run through the rain on their graves,

                        the sky falling
through a crack of light as I talked

                    behind the backs
of everyone who flashed against the dark
    where people live again,

putting a face to small-talk my memory makes.
I can still find between them

                a boy,
a number to a telephone,

                and I know enough to answer
should any of the dead wish to ask
    after Quilla and Cornelia,

or to keep quiet and listen,
let each one tell the story for herself.

        Some night I would like to hear
what our indecent neighbor,
                Otho,

                had to say with his horn,
try to find some hope for the future,

  get a feeling for the love of the blues
even the dead can't put to rest.

CLARE WAS TWELVE WHEN THEY UNEARTHED HER
			one day in the winter woods,
		the beautiful brunette
		girlchild of the veterinarian,
						murdered,

strange in her own shallow grave.

Clare,
		when you were seven
					you raised your hand,

		asking our third grade teacher
	if porcupines threw their quills.
						Bespeckled,

		in a brown dress
	at the front of the room, Miss Griffin retorted,
"Of course."

		Behind you that day in class I had my doubts,
	for ten feet to the right and through the windows

		the seventh April of our lives
	was pouring into the room.

Who is there to trust at such heights?

			Knowing as you do
		that just past those windows

		the swings on the playground facing
	another beginning to winter

and the yellow stucco school
         framed to stand against the generations

have been deserted for twenty years,

Clare, I hope you are glad now to escape
                 the yellow window shades,

    gone,

  no longer having doubts about the world.

There is a story I cannot tell,
                    neither embracing love

      nor pulling far enough from pain,
          although it is true. By 1963,

my father and mother had begun to live by threats
            of getting out for good.

      Silence was hard on everyone,
relieved at night by television as my mother took her cue

      from watching *Perry Mason,*
my father, *Gunsmoke.*

        Then,
     the past was as far from life as the stars,

        and I could take measure of our losses,
find my way back to everywhere I had been,

the way the November day
came when Kennedy was killed and a mockingbird in Alabama

divided into joy
and sang the last of his life entirely away.

It does not matter if the dead live again.
I have found in my blood the direction the brown

leaves blow,
and, like a stairwell,

a light grows out of the story of my life.
I want to hear the mockingbird make her run

while another door opens to a room
that can find no rest on the earth,

a room centering on a black-and-white tv,
taking in the story dispersed from the night

Lyndon Johnson took the oath in the air over Texas,
the sky pushing all brightness against the ground.

Now with my right hand,
I cross my fingers for luck and wish for my friends,

a sign the young president understands,
smiling down as he does from his circling black Continental

as though the earth were personal

and would give anything to take us back again.

Once
          in a Washington museum, between flights,

I walked right up to what I liked
about the anticipation of hyenas

closing in on a porcupine. The porcupine, cornered
  in the glass case, was caught

  taking his last step away from being torn apart.
He didn't throw his quills.

        The hyenas were too close to the kill
  and he needed more

than what he could or could not do to live.

In 1920 there was a secret in Alabama
to pine trees
            letting go their cones

  like chains wrapped tightly
  around gold watches. That was the year

  on the side of the country
  opposite us, Yogananda,

a wise man from India, arrived
in California, teaching the West to fast

  and find happiness.
              His eyes still smile
in the old photographs.

That year my mother
named after the actress
                    still played in the dirt yard,

    never out of sight
    of the house. The world

    was catching its breath between wars,
    there was the old story
                    of the wind through the fields,

and, wherever the daylight took,
goldenrod spread.
                Where I come from there was only one

    reason not to eat what we did
    not have: enlightenment,

a way my people had of recognizing all
they did not live for, their next meal

the revenge tomorrow will take on their prayers.

Back then
I rode on the daylight inside everyone,

    the home I was born to
    not yet made. Between my eyes

there was a star,
a third eye I followed.

Even today
folks have their own way
                    of looking at things

    in every little town in Dixie,
    California still further than most people think.

ONCE THE WINTER CHILD WITHIN ME SAW
a soul extend the golden skin of her wings,

although I chose to ignore my father's good advice
                    to just leave well enough alone,

    and, at the college in the hills beside the frozen creek,
I was shut up

        by an instantly unforgettable teacher
        who wouldn't hear another word.

Something was in the air
                    I didn't need explaining.

            I have to say
William Jay Smith was wrong to turn on me

like a trout striking in the creek,
                    bright and rainbowed

            with earning a living out of where he was.
    I confess I asked too many questions,

                    although
               I considered it more
like every day having something to show for all I kept becoming.

Nothing I said amounted to much
                              but I got away with something

     greater than the emptiness that never leaves
well enough alone.
               A better instructor was the sky

          beyond the creek
     where the stars appeared to have had all the answers.

Across my life
             I know the difference the day-to-day makes.

          I have borrowed from my life's work
     so much I admit
          this must be who I am: a man

who is trying to stop looking over his shoulder,
                    no different from other men

   looking for something new to take care of the past and future,
whatever happens all at once.

               Even now there is something I like
          about Professor Smith

     not taking my tedious questions
     and the way he had when he had enough.

I've learned how hard the answers can be.
                                    But

there is still the one question I have
            concerning whether enough is really enough

    or is there more than meets the eye. Professor Smith,
        do you have any questions for the sky?

Listen. The first line must break out,
        an opening seam down

    to the small pieces of driftwood,
    or the smooth stones your son brings

            from the water in the second line
        that you keep to load
with gifts you've thrown away.
        The splash we hear beneath us

        tells that the dark has an end somewhere

    we must wait to understand.
    January in the third and fourth lines takes us in,

and the fifth allows that you are lost again

        along the water's edge.
                        By now,

in the folding of things, the pond
is still. It's your father by the sixth

    that holds us there,
                    calling you by the water.

The seventh is toward us, friendly but firm:
you are all he sees.
                    With the end becoming

        the beginning again,
         let us know what brought us there,

what takes you back. The conclusion
is by choice —
                notes you keep to yourself,

the son you touch with a free hand,
                            or your father

    as he found you
with us, this time only to say goodbye.

Finally,
let the words be our own shadow

        you stand and leave us in.
        We should see your son to the edge

            and the desk before you shining
            in the clear light, the present

    you are beginning to bring together in the things
    you need around you from this world.

Everette maddox,
   hair still parting on the right and your black beard

over-running the same brown tweed
             and pipe, have you come

                   back to life looking professorial

to find if there is anywhere to go where respect comes with the
                                             job?
             Harvard? Hell?

             You are no more invisible now
than when you lived the life of the mind.

I must tell you I no longer trust the Department of English
             or even the dawn to release

                   some new beginning,
some fresh start of belonging. Or have you come
             back in anger to scare your friends,

                   believing everyone
   but you had gotten laid? I would like to look

around and find you at my side or help you to your home
             on some unrelenting Monday like this
                   burdened with desire in the wind
tearing leaves across the college lawn. Or is home for you now
             as it has always been,

                   everywhere you cannot find again?
Does autumn still fire you with an air of nostalgia

for pure youth? Remember the years with promise
in Tuscaloosa, those fierce colleagues you cursed

                    who charged headlong into careers?
What were they looking for?
                              From where you stand is it possible

            for a man to live
        safely with his writing? Read to me again the only poem

I ever understood, the one that makes me
        remember to follow, to listen and not to speak.

            Teachers, friends,
maybe the dead live again in the lives they changed.
                Does the richness

            of language explain
        the best of ourselves only to cut

us out of the crowd with a heightened sense? I have been
        struggling as much as ever for what refuses to be

            anything
other than the maples' crowded color staggering red to orange.
        So I want you to tell me where you are, Rette.
                Sometimes I see you
        in the moonlight out of style, come badly to the end, alone.

If death is just a way we have of getting there
        I want you to climb into another shape on the other side.

You wanted happiness.
Your heart was suspect. At the last
  you drank Scotch by the fifth and slept in trash.

Homeless,
  your face draws closer when I write,

still trying for the right words to find their way
          into your wish and mine that you were here.

Through stacks of prayers the dead abandon,
  old news and gray breath,

past the reel of blood in its shells,
  blood in clouds and boats full of rain,

where do the angels freeze into time,

  cold hands, lovers the color of storms,

    where do they begin to care?

Words tuck under their own wings,
  those that nights churn,
    those crows cry beyond their simple strength,

  recital of my hands,

    change my throat to words,

my flesh to flesh.

Why should I hope the breath stronger
        when nothing will be raised unchanged?

        I remember snow falling through falling snow
whitens the next life.

        I remember the sea crawls across itself
                grateful to no one.

We do what we can for the dead.
We don't give the dead a second thought.

Heaven for heaven, whatever closes turns back flowering:

    how dust parts for the soul
and how it holds you and why it matters.
        Someday you will know winds

yearning and haunting the sky.   Dust holds you,
        blood under all music.

And the sky tells your story; it points,
        web in the sky,
clouds following the veils the hand opens and sifts.

It's not the future with its yellow hue
It's not the footprints asking the way
It's not in sleep's velvet syllable
        Nor in astronomy drying its web
Not the resurrected in their bare tree

It's autumn lost leaf to leaf again
        It's the riddle breath studies
A long time turning blue

It's finally I'll mistake sleep
    And lose the body
Passed from hand to hand through stone

    Out and back out and unreachable
        the fly forgets
    her sonata rising from its ashes

I'd be wildflowers

a life summer flames awake and would be lightened of

    But I'm here,
    and how will it be
    that loose assembly of landslides?

Time divides sleep from its open window
    cave-shaped
        to divide the self

why the moon of three faiths is so blue and cold
        constellations hidden in the true name of snow

in salt and the sun. In lip and water.
In choices living makes and promises it keeps.

The river has no place.
    Where the crone in a white gown sweats over the body,
    where the old man drives a roaring hammer
        into the snow and frozen ground,

this grave shifts side to side;

        what is tied now

to breath and river

shifts side to side.

Sing alone, down and down, and lie down
to drink your swift face from the water.

How many gods
                              cry suddenly together,

   wing of the heart
beating skyward on its back?

      How many mouth
      the word the newborn keeps,

that one name he cries back as he begins to forget?

   Chill rising into breath
      and my blood remembering
   how walking at night

   into the body heat of that barn

   was another kind of light

      my blood remembering
   how the smell
      in dark hay of horses and cattle

   standing asleep held to my breath
   was warm brown bread rising

Sunrise

God confusing the mockingbird with the unicorn

   Less and less
     human wing

mockingbird tell me who

     who left the cradle of sea
      of stars in my hands

Mockingbird throw my voice away
   pitch it through the curtains
    and windows of my hands

    before I sleep

before I know my faith as a handful of hours

before I take the wind's shape and claim the earth's webbed
                       names.

    I awake once more

    weather   voice   hand   hair

I awake once more into the future's architecture of gravity

   and know

 why this planet is circling,

why this day rounds me with stone and rain.

Nothing to do but reassemble the body

A year of burials   Put that behind us   Come

It is enough
to touch our mouths together

allowing the parable to speak

its pitch pine and skeletal phosphorescent motions

When I go, when I return, spent,

my words stained and lost, blue and unfamiliar,

what language will I hear
in fire,
in hope
drawn through thousands of years?

What will I give into the strength pressed against me,

the guardians putting down their white hymns,
track of the sun and moon?

DEEP IN THE LUNGS OF GRAVES
hides a nerved diamond of light,
  a little wooden bridge
we'll hold hands crossing,

in the inaudible vowels of stars filling their bare tree,

and the moon . . . and the white slave of the moon.

What was it
        there on asphalt among parked cars

    that I could be blinded
  walking out of the hospital doors,
                        turning to see
    the sun take the windows on every floor apart

in the Monday of the first hour of my son's birth,
                                blinded

      by his changing my life
    that, all these years,
        had been trying to right itself,

that was breaking now into shrill breath?

  I hold my own head in my hands,
the same unpronounceable cradle

song of nothingness gradually giving him over, raising his cries.

  On the night my son slept,

                    divided from the unborn by one

dawn and the end

             the Talladega forest makes of the power
    road, I walk into scrub

pine and red oak I know like my own
               body, climb out

   the valley that falls through the Warrior
  river, crackle a small fire out of fatpine,

and watch the dead
       pass hand to hand through the flames.

     Over my head a hawk

   rides his guttural and highstrung questions,
                his cry

   splintering
      beyond the thin pines:

Why do you not open your mouth?
Through all your cravings
         can you not find your way to glide
     motionless
        out of the depth
and ground of your bone-hunting life?

       I huddled
and heard the future hoarding its clocks,
          saw thunderheads

    glut

the faint east.

I slept. I was a boy in his grave
so dawn became a boy on his knees, catching

and kicking a ball. He kicked
and the ball came back
from the other side that holds the ground.
He waited and the ball fell back,

blue
in the arc that rose with the ball and rose.

The way it works is this:
it's being narrow-minded about the hillside. It's working

my way in,
staying stupid enough to lose

my mind, to keep
changing it like a skin that grows with me.
It's being awake enough to keep moving the same place.

It's not running. It's not turning
my back on anything that stands.

It's expecting no one
then waiting for them to arrive.

It's looking ahead and taking
nothing, calling it mine when it is out of my hands.

Claiming the dazzled cries
                    that open the voice of my son,

    cracked, infinite, split,

            the earth as it is,
I fly with the hawk the broken after-image of the Appalachian,

        descending through the shapes of rivers into my son's birth,

            stretched in my mind

    between latitudes

            where the blue whale's slack eye
            is the enthralled glare of God.

            Having been herded out of heaven,
God is dying in the condor's wingspan

        deepening already to a final wildness.

And through the shrill
                    birthing of our kind

    He embraces us in the rough of all creation

while the blue whale swells toward Him like the east.

As though I were eating
                    the insides of my own body,

          my mouth
     fills with salt,

          passing through
the wandering of whales into their vast inflammable lives,

     our minds together in the sun
          like an hourglass with no shape.

     Out of our mouths the same
     breath fills with a cry of birth

          whose sole pleasure is to rise
and bear witness. With my borne son

I lie down beside the blue whale as beside the moon,

     the way the son I was
          streams into the father I am,

     the whale
          taking from me my animal

     shape,
and I can no longer find my own face crossed with my son's.

     Out of nakedness I grow into the sea,
     a whole eternal presence

shedding the cry of my son until over my head it reaches
the ocean's blue calm like a mountain fleeing upward.

Even the dead move from underground to the floor of the sea,

                              something I am
       becoming,
              drawing breath on its own.

I hear the points of rain falling in separate voices

              on skin
       the water makes of water.

       The whale whirls through the dead
who long
       for the hammering of themselves to begin again.

       I cannot see
but something like sight touches

       the paw of the timber wolf,
              the yellow claw of the condor,

hears their long howls

   thrown on the run through the sky.
Beginning as I never could be

   but am —
in a Galilee of great eggs nesting in cliffs —

I know I will never die.

              The whale's scattering cry,
   holding me like an ocean turning to kindness,

40

stands out
in a long grain of mercy like the sun,

            and, as I open my mouth,
    I speak the whale's strengthcurving wish.

    In the sea
    I am as cold as the cry the whale keeps making

                colder than the water,
        making me another

                            thing from the end of light.
The cry of the whale is taking the shape of muscular wanting.

    Supple and released in the howl of the wolf,
            the joy of the unborn

    breaks up the terrifying postures of the sea,
crying to my son and feeling his heart's

        simple gesture toward the eternal,
a valley beginning to open in the name of God.

        At my own edge,
    just before the second coming of human speech,

    in the water my son leaves
        leaving his mother,

the tremendous bones of the Messiah of the blue whale
                        fall
    like a tree of blood,
and I breathe back the crowded cries of my kind.

WHEN WILBUR JACKSON TOOK THE PITCHOUT
at the Crimson Tide 20

          he rolled
        with the backfield to the short side,

        seemed to hesitate,
                  almost drift

          before spinning completely around the first man
      who tried to take him,

          began to glide up the sideline
        near the Bear

            then blew past the Tennessee secondary.
      In those nine seconds

        did not something irreversible occur?

        As a slave's grandson's son raised
      seventy thousand indifferent men to their feet

            in a spontaneous roar,
      it was not that the uncoiled fire hoses of Birmingham

            were repelled,
        or that the dark and shallow delta graves

        rose
      in unrequited light,

or that in the passing of one hundred and eight years
        the cast-iron chokers and the balls and chains

            suddenly lost their grip on the earth.
    Yet, did not

                this man at nineteen,
        across eighty yards that were all white

until he tucked the football under his left arm
                                and ran

            through one long cry of pleasure,

                did he not take on something more?
Did he not run once, out of his life, to join

            the invisible together like a prayer,
                        to be skin

        the words themselves had grown?
For a time the flesh of the Word was

                                his flesh.
He stepped out of time and held it against himself

as though running along the Eastern edge of the holy
            past where all life can go

        without being made again,
            while the earth held

        close to his every move under the lights,
    held pale and blue and glorious,

held to the dead and to the living
    in downward drawn and nuclear time.

       Was he not,
    leaving everyone twenty yards behind him,

   more than a man,

  having taken hold of something larger
and entered the form of a world that was not his own

     so completely
    it became his possession?

Was he not for that moment a god?

The year John Kennedy was shot
     I tried to measure the speed of light.

  A little motor
  in a clumsy pine box hummed

          and sank
    a beam of light into mirrors and prisms.

The effort was to track between distant places an equation
the light left. I never got it.
          The prisms missed. The motor
  quit, and the pine box that held it all,

  that I remember believing
was like the flat-black stern guiding fallen heroes

over the Styx and out of the world

through the *Iliad* that year in school,

                              fell apart.

         A judge complained, "There's no logic to it."

I do not remember why the whole device never made it
              back home from the fair, although it won,
                out of respect, I suppose, for aspiration.
It's odd

         how time and memory settle themselves,
    shimmering quickly or slowly into something new:
               the future without the dead.

                 If the dead wanted,

the end that holds us back would be nothing less

         than heaven, a redefinition of shape. We stand alone
    on this side of the river the sky becomes

    and are no longer children,

                              while time cracks
over memory telling its own story so that it might

         better resemble us and become what we think of
              as hope

              that often like light
seems to arrive from some distance to claim us.

In the stern of the green boat
                          my father guides

            over the muscle of the Chattahoochee
along bream beds and fern-choked shade,

        I am taking him at his words:
                fish draw to silence.

        And as he points my next cast
over the cold silver afternoon I arch my wrist

    not as we practiced standing in dry grass
            but a wrong way,

            lashing the line's arc
        and the tiny bronze plow of the hook to touch

    my father's brown eye.
                        His left eye bleeding,

he is pointing again to where the first one is taking
                                the hook

            like a handshake and descending,
the strange yellow underbelly larger than my palm,

        the wide eyes exacting
        the same endlessness as the river's sheen.

Going home,
my father can hardly contain his joy, his eyes quiet.

I do not remember how it heals
but it does. The sun

had burned only my right arm,
porchlights begin crowding the edges of fields,

the car is
warm,

and the waters, filling
with fog, are fit to the light of the world.

Because of the death of our fathers
we look down into our hands

and our hands are like stones we place between
ourselves and the dead.

Because the death of our fathers
we become

the fathers our sons make of us,
stories so complete
they overflow into the final, inexhaustible figures.

THE CHOCTOW ALONG THE CHATTAHOOCHEE
held legends that are only grass now.
They have forgotten for whom the living shout.

Under stars that have no names
they have forgotten

the thin dugouts of their graves.
Now behind running lights

slow coal barges

trudge downriver with their tugs,

Mae Forrest, Dixie Darling, Sweet Geraldine,
and are gone.

Those of us remaining will always believe the dead
burn

like a house falling in around us.
They know our names

are like stars,
fire flying over the living,

our names that must not be spoken until they have lost their way.

East of the air

my grandmother and grandfather lie side to side while
their fierce church stands ready,

                        behind them
            and looking elsewhere now.

        To the west my grandmother is
    still eleven, asleep in her father's arms.

    They are taking their time getting to the sky,

                its bridge
            a quarter mile,

        a quarter moon away.
                    My grandfather is still playing his fiddle.

        He is nearly dancing now,
    a farmer leaving nothing beneath these

                    trees that held his slow fields together,
    fields that did not last.

                He forgets what is tied to memory,
                and forgets to sing

        as around them and over my head

    a mockingbird takes the half-spent voice of everything around
                                            her.

        So let us confuse the mockingbird with faith

    the things hoped for
                laying a shape to her song

    Let her fill the unborn

                        the night and the day

with her vertical   her empty   her hurtling song

            Let the mockingbird say something indivisible

                    simple

                    free-falling

                and standing out

like a single grain of light in the first minutes of the day

            Is it possible to believe that opposite any song
now at a shrine in hell,
                            hired hands,
                                        night-watchmen,
                                                    the last
of the sharecroppers' sons wearing silk more
                    expensive than their wives' clothes

                could raise a flag of sorts,
        a cross of two-by-fours,

and could hold one another the way children might,

                their hoods and frocks
            like the masque of children, that those men might lead

one of their kind into that closing circle
                                    and one by one

raise him, nailing

his open palms onto the cross that stands in fire before it falls?

Sunday, and my father has not raised his voice
to silence us,

all boys, tired from the day
in Tutweiler Prison for women.

He steers the bus filled with summer
behind the picture windshields,

wipers as long as my legs. Beneath the floorboard
the road home shakes.

Out of the side windows fields unravel.
This

I will learn
is solitude that parallels farm country

and fills the twilight falling with slow loveliness.
Soon there is just a sense of full ground.

I can still hear the steel doors rattle like trains.

On their own

they open and close

                    and we are left
                              facing the dark eyes of women.

        That night
       in bed I woke myself crying,

the brown bread of their bodies unending and sweet in the air.

It filled the whole indoors.
                              But in bed

   fire rose through my screams, a tree burned

               black in an open field
     where the door to my room stood closed,
           my mother caught there, flecked and cracked,

     my father against her, flecked and cracked in the tree-
   shedding caves of fire the tree became, my mother

              holding to the ground
                flames tore through,

        my father without arms to catch her,
        silent,
calm.
        Around them
                    flames mocked poses of the human,
like women I had seen on all the crowded floors,

     my mother flamed open, burned like bread, gone,
     my father, gone, the fire burning down,

my bed black

and filled with crying

                                    and I woke
like a ghost suddenly set loose from shapelessness.

  I came to myself in my mother's arms.
               To my father's voice
  I woke in a house crowded wholly with light.

On my father's shoulders
                    I probed the night sky,

    trying to understand a point of light
rounding the summer,

          having finished
supper, having gone with our neighbors onto the lawns,

          not to miss
    what none had seen, something unavoidably there,

a satellite, *Sputnik,*
                    too fast to be a star,

    found out heading over the Atlantic.

Tonight I cradle and walk my son
               gathered completely into living air,

          mumble an old story

of a rocket crossing the Milky Way to a slight people
          who seemed to me

in my father's telling
a proof of God.

Through interstellar ridges where hope
once burned like pride,

I take my father's voice
and throw it to one asleep at last in my arms.

The watermarks time leaves around my eyes
are deepening

and I can run my finger along the crease of skin, that good luck
I keep surviving;

no better map to guide the divinities
from one of us to the other

without more fuss
than these crow's feet.

And where would an angel step into time but here?

What is this image that for one more day was without end?

Are not these their faces jammed together,
reflected and transparent in the glare,

deforming me with their subtle defamations?

I know nothing is unforgiving
and would like to believe
in a flowering—but my face has lost clarity.
It is beginning to drift through itself.

I want to take hold of what stays.
I would like to hold the child I was the way I am learning

     how to hold my son
            who, like the world,

   is blameless, and not sure he understands.

Driving at night, my headlights balance against the land.

         We speed forward,
      draining,
   on clear nights like this, into spirals
         exchanged for sleep,

then, later, distance: the good time we make.
Like everyone, I have a single story.
            In December,

    the asylum sealed and filled with steam, still
       dark, I climbed the steel

      fire escape to a kitchen's back door,
       one hand on the cold rail,

   opened,
       slammed the cold out,

startling Henry McDonald.
      Henry, having killed a wife and son once,
        turned from dressing
slabs of pork in the dark kitchen to raise one hand

above his head,
flinging that cleaver that wheeled, once,

before its handle-end struck the soft length of my chest,
driving me down.

It is difficult for me to explain to anyone
his strength,
his suddenness,
and why I let him take up the knife nearly at my feet,

why I could not kick him away,
already holding the cleaver by its blade

as we spilled across the floor.
Now,

eighteen years later,
head-down and buckled in the back seat,
my small son sleeps. There is little traffic.
As far

as I know Henry McDonald died years ago

in peace he found past the end.

Yet I did not know his loss as it fit a final form against me:

a split in that distance
between one end of the knife

and daylight taking the road ahead.

my wife turns from the car to the house
with its green magnolia,

while in the distance a pony appears and is chased
by neighbor girls,

E'lan, Ariel,
in red and blue caps.

And what is right about time and memory
is that the pony, Jim,

understanding
the outstretched hands and pears

to be a figure for love,
and reward for keeping still,

consents to being caught, just as the magnolia,

releasing its oval leaves,

surrounds us.

This grace, the messenger said is blood.

Hear her out.

            Is suck and wash of light.

This,

        the messenger said, is dust.

                            These are the works of your body
            pointing around the sky.

    Halo and glitter, this grace is ash
                the gray code you live by.

        Have you not found it in fire?
            In the scrawling of a few pine logs?

    Think of me as fire.

    Can you not hear your soul?

Is not your heart on its back
                a better wing beating skyward?

                The dead believe
they find God in the underbelly of the leaf print.

        They try to float west with the sun.

        Have you not heard them praying?

    I want to give in to the strength pressed against me.

I want the guardians to put down their hymns
                where madness takes no shape

and even the stones under my feet
howl.
        Where the fear I seize
                is some resemblance beyond my knowing,

        beyond the stars that turn their back to me

I know water is the father of magic and mother of God.

                As we enter

    we are filled.

            I call the last angel to sing

                    of how with the dead

            he will bleed into the earth's side,
how he will stand in my place in the sun, a human shadow
        where shadows are

                        the blind guides of the world,
the silhouettes of divinities.

I want him to close his mouth and turn face down against me.

        Out of the clear sky
I heard a calling past the deepest trees. *Not so far,* I said.

    Not too close, he answered.
                        On this hand

a flock of starlings left the night wide open.

Not so high,

someone shouted.

Not so far, I said.

On the other hand sycamores took the black moon

in their arms

above a ring of red tails, run of starlings,

circling, calling, around and around.

Not too close, they shouted.

Not so far, I said.

FOR YOU, STEPHEN,
I want to throw the dead

out
who keep dawning in our features.

I want to hold these words close to your face.

The dark shaped out of your mother

became your heart

and your heart still flings

its one wave
over waters from her world.

Slick, cosmic, whole,
when you were born before my eyes,

        when you bore your mother back into herself,
                        the air took you,

and I think I understood for once the nerve-endings of faith,

        why my hours could lose
                        their way,
why even the laws quiver behind one another,

                and the dead can't fail us.
        I knew how the rain makes full confession,

understood how the beginning is not the end,

        how stars milk the open spaces,

        why mercy is bewildering.

                        I give you
the winter alive in each dawn, for your eyes are blue wells.

                I give you your mother's name
that is the name for the moon with its mouth to the ground.

        Aperture of salt,
                little horse of God,

                        I hold you
through the night that is some ridiculously opposite and solar
        promise

while the weather prepares and unprepares the sea opening and
closing,

while all about us the invisible grows
arctic with time.

I have come to know my madness
    as a torn and empty wonder

  a dancing eye
    flying like the ghost of a stone

I have come to know angels

  bones of the air

    their prayer swinging on its chain

  angels God contrived
   hung from His silver hair

 to know the wings' slow expansion
   to realize more,
crows crowded out of the apple tree,

  angels riding His impossible light

  a candle's numberless masks

Foxglove, who watches me as I dream,
explosions of blue in ruined plumes blowing open.

   And the words wander away on their own.

The end is the smallest well
                    singing
    and there is no beginning
claiming to be a cave,

                the first man dawning,
        woman stepping from her curtain of wounds,
            the just-born.

    I want to open my eyes.

    I want to stare from a deep well,
        I want to witness the stranger here,
        watch him draw water

                    from my throat.

        I want my soul to drag its one leg,

    a candle's spent motion

        I want to draw

                    drink deeply

    I want to hear the deep nothing calling my name.